Primary

Professional

Development

Improving Pupil Achievement through Target Setting

Roger Smith

Acknowledgements

The author would like to thank all the many people who have contributed directly and indirectly to the thinking that has culminated in this book:

- all those course and conference members who have helped, often without knowing, to shape the ideas expressed here
- the staff and governors of Milverton Primary School
- his wife and children for their patience
- Chris Reeve and Elaine Brown.

The author also acknowledges his debt to Warwickshire's team of inspectors for their publication *Target Setting in Schools* (Warwickshire Education Department, 1998) from which the material on pp.59–63 is taken.

Editor: Karen Westall   Layout artist: Suzanne Ward
Illustrations: Eric Jones   Cover design: Ed Gallagher
Cover image: 'Indian Boy', George Catlin

© 2000 Folens Limited, on behalf of the author.

Every effort has been made to contact copyright holders of material used in this book. If any have been overlooked, we will be pleased to make any necessary arrangements.

British Library Cataloguing in Publication Data. A catalogue record for this book is available from the British Library.

First published 2000 by Folens Limited, Dunstable and Dublin.
Folens Limited, Albert House, Apex Business Centre, Boscombe Road, Dunstable, LU5 4RL, England.

ISBN 1 86202 986–5

Printed in Singapore by Craft Print

Contents

Introduction and key themes

There is nothing more important to teachers, parents and pupils than raising standards of achievement. This is a fundamental part of a vision of excellence for all schools and it means setting achievable but challenging targets that will help to improve pupils' attainments.

One extremely important way that achievement in primary education is measured is by attainment in the national tests at the end of Key Stage 1 and Key Stage 2. In some schools, the publication of the results of the national tests and their conversion into league tables by the local and national press has created a climate of anxiety and tension.

This book is aimed at teachers and schools who want to make the most of themselves through improvements. It will suggest straightforward ways of setting targets and discuss various useful strategies to raise achievement in a general sense as well as specifically to improve national test results.

What is the book about?

How to raise achievement

✔ Firstly, it is important that target setting is understood and managed and that it is seen by all teachers to be a useful tool in raising achievement.

✔ Secondly, there must be a whole-school approach to improving results and raising achievement. No individual class teacher is an island and one centre of excellence in a sea of mediocrity will not raise standards. There has to be a common knowledge base of how to use assessments to raise expectations as well as a whole-school approach to creating a high quality team of teachers who can work effectively together.

✔ Thirdly, improving test results and raising achievement will not just occur by chance, or because the headteacher and governors order it to happen or the parents want it to occur. It has to be planned and schemes of work, lesson plans and teaching styles have to help to move each teacher and each pupil towards improving achievement.

✔ Fourthly, there are techniques that can be used and adapted by teachers, subject co-ordinators and headteachers that will not only work in making improvements but will help to overcome any barriers to raising achievement that are encountered.

Aims of the book

This book will be useful to teachers, co-ordinators and headteachers and, as such, will provide a highly accessible resource that is both practical and meaningful.

At the same time, the ideas are there to be used to support and guide all the initiatives to improve pupil achievement and test results that are in place in individual schools.

Each chapter should inspire and encourage a whole-school culture of improvement and provide techniques and skills that will enable teachers not only to improve the test results of their pupils but to strengthen the value of improving achievement. By doing this, they should also begin to remove the barriers that exist which prevent improvement from taking place.

What does improving achievement mean?

School improvement is defined largely in terms of outcomes that demonstrate higher standards of attainment, with particular emphasis on literacy and numeracy in national tests at age seven and eleven. Improvement in these tests has to occur alongside the statutory requirement for children to be given access to a broad and balanced curriculum. It is becoming more and more important, however, for schools to make sure that the basic skills within the core subjects of English, Maths and Science are seen to be improving, or at the very least are reflecting the abilities of the pupils in the school.

How to make improvements

Making improvements has got to involve:

- ✔ setting clear and appropriate targets within all other subjects including ICT
- ✔ developing effective teaching skills
- ✔ creating better assessments
- ✔ using these assessments to improve the quality and content of teaching
- ✔ setting clear learning objectives
- ✔ planning to make sure that these teaching and learning objectives are met.

How will improvements be measured?

The DfEE/OFSTED (1996) booklet *Setting Targets to Raise Standards: A Survey of Good Practice* states: 'Schools should monitor their performance regularly with the aim of identifying and taking specific action to raise standards of achievement. They should set clear targets, appropriate to their own circumstances and build them into any post inspection action plan and school development plan.' (p.7)

Tests and levels

All children entering school have to be tested using base line assessment and, as has already been suggested, they are then tested again at age seven and eleven. It is possible to examine raw scores in all these tests year on year and reach conclusions about whether the pupils are attaining appropriate levels. Teachers will be able to use test levels and scores using other tests in Years 3, 4 and 5 to predict achievements, or more accurately set targets that are realistic for their pupils. Such targeting should make for better focused teaching, the more effective use of resources and clearer objectives for the pupil.

School improvement can also be measured against base line levels to find out the extent to which a school has 'added value' to its pupils' learning. The amount of value added is the fairest way of assessing a school's performance and comparing it with that of other schools. This is important because, as well as recognising improvements and higher achievements in individual schools, it is useful to be able to compare schools with similar catchment areas, similar levels of special needs pupils and any other measurable comparisons.

How can benchmarking help?

Benchmarking is the process of measuring standards of actual performance in one school against those achieved by other schools with broadly similar characteristics.

Amongst a group of schools sharing similar characteristics, the benchmark represents the standard of performance achieved by the best members of the group and indicates what should be achievable by all the similar schools. In its simplest terms, it gives contextual information against which to set realistic tasks for improvement.

Schools should try to avoid looking at their results and making generalised comparisons with no attempt at setting the context within which the results were achieved. If they do this they will mask the widely differing results achieved by similar intakes of pupils and the fact that some schools appear far more successful than others in helping pupils to achieve their full potential.

What questions should schools be asking?

✔ Why is it that some schools like ours can achieve results which appear so much better?
✔ What are these schools doing from which we can learn?
✔ What progress can we make to achieve similar results?
✔ How can we plan that progress and over what period of time?

Once some of the answers to the general questions have started to suggest ways forward and the changes that are necessary, it is important to develop a staged plan that will, if it is successful, guarantee improved achievement. The part of the plan that is suggested below is in five stages. It will form part of the following chapters and will be used as a framework for development in Chapter 6.

> ## A five-stage plan for school improvement
>
> Consider the following five questions:
>
> ✔ How well are we doing? (Look at our own scores against our own targets and our own past scores.)
>
> ✔ How do we compare with similar schools?
>
> ✔ What should we aim to achieve next year?
>
> ✔ What have we got to do to make this happen?
>
> ✔ When we check future results, will we be able to say that we have made a difference and will we be able to identify precisely what made that difference?

Using assessment information

It is in the subjects of English, Maths and Science that National Curriculum test and assessment data are available, that other tests, such as norm referenced standardised tests, are more likely to be produced and that tests in Years 3 to 5 are obtainable. All schools use the same tests and, therefore, have the same data obtainable. It is important that subject managers or co-ordinators are involved in looking at test results in their subjects and that they have the time, the skills and the support to be able to analyse them critically and effectively with a view to future improvements.

Key questions

There are several key questions which the analysis of assessment data might help teachers to answer:

✔ How is our school currently performing overall in these specific subjects?

✔ Are some classes more effective than others?

✔ Are some key stages more effective than others?

✔ Are some parts of individual subjects better or worse than others, such as reading within English, mental arithmetic within Maths?

✔ Are some groups of pupils doing better than others, for example boys versus girls, or different ethnic groups?

✔ How do achievements in the subject now compare with previous achievements?

✔ How does our school's performance in each subject compare with that of other schools?

What can the whole school do?

A corporate approach

First of all, it is important to remember that improving achievement, raising standards and achieving higher test scores demands a whole-school effort that involves all leaders, especially headteachers and co-ordinators. No-one should be expected to, or can, achieve this alone and certainly no-one should be required to take sole responsibility for raising standards.

We have already suggested that individual subject co-ordinators have an important role to play, and this will be discussed in later chapters, but within the school's own cycle of development, there should be processes and action plans written into the School Development Plan to influence and improve achievement directly.

Time has to be set aside to discuss achievement, to plan for change and to work out exactly what to do as a whole school, using whole-school discussions and information as well as that provided by subject co-ordinators.

Answering all the questions, however, will not in itself move a school forward in terms of successful improvements. The effectiveness of any raising-achievement initiative will depend on the consistency with which it is applied and the accuracy with which its effectiveness is evaluated. Once again, this must be seen as a whole-school issue which needs both long- and short-term objectives.

Scores and more scores as short-term objectives

The introductory paragraph of this chapter reminded us that primary league tables are no longer officially published, but the information upon which the tables were constructed still is. National and local newspapers construct their own league tables which, according to some newspapers in March 1999, 'galvanise' primary schools, make 'compelling' reading, are part of a drive to 'raise standards' and yet, at the same time, can present a 'distorted' picture of a school's true worth. The fact that they are seen to be newsworthy makes them important public documents which cannot be treated either with contempt or disdain.

However, they do have problems. These are the main ones:

✔ They are only raw statistics which fail to take into account the background of the pupils.
✔ They only show the percentage of pupils reaching the 'expected level'. The proportion of pupils achieving better than this, i.e. Level 3 at age seven and Level 5 at age eleven, is not recorded.
✔ Pupils absent for any tests are treated statistically as if they had failed to reach Level 4.
✔ Special needs pupils who are exempt from the tests are also treated statistically as if they had failed to reach Level 4.

'My only regret is that my absence will depress the school's position in the league tables.'

But in spite of these areas of doubt, the results are widely available and it is in the school's interest to obtain the best possible results from their pupils. Educational improvement is a key government focus and this is obviously what schools want for all their pupils.

It is easy to say but less easy to achieve, but it should be the aim of all primary schools and primary teaching to raise standards and improve achievement. To do this needs successful teachers in effective schools working to improve the quality of teaching and learning and working to reduce the barriers that limit an individual child's and the school's achievements.

Setting appropriate targets

The purpose of target setting is to ensure that each pupil is given the opportunity to achieve his or her potential, both academically and in other areas of school life. It has also been accepted as a major tool for school improvement and, because of this, it is important that the target setting process both helps individual pupils and meets the needs of the school's overall plan for raising achievement.

Legislation on target setting

We need to make one thing perfectly clear. There is no escape from *target setting*. It is a fact of school life. Rather than spending time criticising its effect on attainment or the amount of time it takes to set targets, individual teachers and schools need to develop a process that works and that will be part of their overall drive to raise standards.

Publications

The DfEE publication *Setting Targets to Raise Standards* suggested that 'setting targets for pupil attainment enabled schools to measure their progress against *clear aims and planned outcomes*' (p.4) (my italics). In 1996, Sir Ron Dearing and Sir Peter Davis, Chairman of the National Advisory Council for Education and Training Targets (NACETT), proposed a revised national framework for target setting and presented a case for the government to adopt national school targets to underpin it.

In 1997, the Labour Government published two more relevant documents: its White Paper, *Excellence in Schools*, which proposed targets for each of the key stages of statutory schooling, and *From Targets to Action*, which offered guidance to schools on how to support effective target setting. SCAA also issued a consultation paper, *Target Setting and Benchmarking*, which made it clear that 'the government saw statutory target setting as forming an *essential but slim core element in a much wider process of target setting and school improvement*' (p.8) (my italics).

Future targets

In autumn 1997, the government set national targets for 11-year-olds in English and Mathematics. By the year 2002, 80% of pupils are expected to attain Level 4 in English and 75% Level 4 in Mathematics. Individual teachers will have to make sure that the standards their pupils achieve help the school to reach its own agreed targets. These, in turn, will inform LEA targets which will help to meet the national targets set for 2002.

The benefits of target setting

Target setting as an approach to raising educational standards establishes specific measurable goals for improved pupil performance. It leads to greater clarity and helps a school to focus on pupil performance. Headteachers can use pupil performance targets to underline priorities that serve as a reminder of where the school is heading. Many aspects of target setting are not new and most teachers in primary schools are already setting targets for individual pupils which usually focus on short-term targets for improvement. It is already seen as a significant strategy for improving the achievement of pupils and needs to fit into a sensible cycle of school review, planning and action.

Advantages

✔ It helps to raise teachers' expectations.
✔ It helps to focus on the potential of individual pupils in a range of areas.
✔ It forces teachers to identify ways to support individual potential.
✔ It sharpens the focus of teachers on whether their teaching is of an appropriate quality.
✔ It allows teachers to examine the relevance and usefulness of their long-, medium- and short-term curriculum planning.
✔ It improves pupils' responsibility for their own learning through discussion of specific targets with individual children and by explaining target setting to parents.
✔ It focuses pupils' attention on how they can improve their learning.

Disadvantages

✔ Teachers are beginning to give the impression to their pupils and to parents that tests and the test subjects are all that matters.
✔ There is an overemphasis on target setting in terms of core subjects.
✔ National tests may reduce the importance and value of knowledge, skills and understanding across the broad swathe of the primary curriculum.
✔ Teachers may unduly focus on 'borderline' pupils to meet a specific target and 'prove' that they have raised achievement in some measurable way.
✔ Concentrating on 'borderline' pupils (and in spring 1999 the government provided 'booster' money for Year 6 pupils who, with extra help, might achieve Level 4 in the national tests) might diminish the need to make sure that all pupils should be enabled to meet their potential.

Obviously target setting has a large part to play in raising achievement, but we must not lose sight of each individual pupil and his or her achievements in all aspects of a broad and balanced curriculum. In order to harness the benefits and avoid the disadvantages, there needs to be a set of principles and some recommended processes that will inform the best use of target setting.

Principles of target setting

The purpose of target setting has to be to raise the achievement and quality of educational achievement for all pupils, with the pupils themselves remaining at the centre of the process. This means raising the achievement of individuals and doing this will, of course, raise the overall achievement of the school, which will be reflected in measurable outcomes such as the national tests at seven and eleven.

Targets

Targets should:

✔ be challenging and raise standards for all

✔ be SMART:
  - Specific
  - Measurable
  - Appropriate and Agreed
  - Realistic and Recorded
  - Time related

✔ take into account the context within which the school and its pupils are working

✔ be based on sound evidence, supported by the school's own evidence and by useful national and LEA benchmarking information

✔ reflect and reinforce priorities in the School Development Plan, inform the LEA Education Development Plan and contribute towards DfEE requirements

✔ meet any statutory requirements but should extend beyond this through the school's own achievement-raising targets and the recognition of achievement in other areas

✔ be set far enough in advance to be meaningful

✔ be monitored regularly

✔ fit into a cycle of school improvement which involves five stages:
  - Analysing current performance
  - Comparing results with similar schools
  - Setting the actual targets
  - Planning the action
  - Taking action and reviewing progress

✔ require a balance of pressure and support for success

✔ be set so as not to disadvantage any individual pupil or group of pupils in order that a school may meet its individual targets

✔ be set in a positive climate created by the headteacher and governing body which overcomes caution.

It has been suggested already in this chapter that the starting point for the target setting process is the current attainment of individual pupils. It is from this point that challenging but realistic targets for each child will be set. The targets for each pupil will contribute to the targets for a cohort of pupils and this, in turn, will contribute to the targets for the school, the LEA and nationally.

Targets and improved performance

Of course, target setting will not improve performance and raise achievement on its own. Schools will have to develop a plan which will bring about the required improvements, such as changes to culture, policy and practice. This clear plan of action will involve:

✔ concerted and rigorous effort
✔ a focus on classroom practice
✔ the appropriate use of resources.

In a sense, this is suggesting that it is important not to spend too much time on forecasting and agreeing the actual targets, since as much time and energy as possible needs to be devoted to the action which will help pupils to achieve the targets and improve their performance.

Forecasting and setting targets

Start with the individual

If the process starts with the individual children, then each teacher needs to consider their current performance, using assessment and other data together with his or her knowledge of the individuals, their rate of progress and factors which might affect their learning.

Each teacher can then forecast what level the pupil is likely to achieve at the end of the next key stage.

What must happen next, of course, is that each teacher must also consider what the pupil could achieve if a real challenge were added, or if, for example, more support or more one-to-one teaching could be provided for that individual.

Make comparisons

At this stage, the forecasts and potential targets will probably be discussed across the age range and with previous teachers. Then, with this wider perspective, comparisons need to be made with the performance of schools with similar cohorts to ensure that the school is setting its sights high enough.

Discuss widely

These aggregated draft targets need to be discussed with the governors and the LEA before they are finalised. But, whilst it is the governors who have the responsibility for 'setting' the targets, the expectation is that the targets are based on an understanding of the current attainment of the pupils in the cohort being considered and on what would be challenging for those pupils.

Review annually

For a variety of reasons, pupils may make more or less progress than expected and it is therefore important to review the targets each year alongside up-to-date test and assessment data, in order to ensure that the targets are still realistic as well as challenging.

The five-stage cycle of school improvement

Target setting should put all aspects of pupils' performance at the centre of the school's work.

The best model for underpinning target setting is one which builds on the processes already used by many schools for school development planning. This five-stage model is circular rather than linear because the process doesn't stop. There is no end to the process but a continuing development from the original starting point of: 'How well are we doing?'

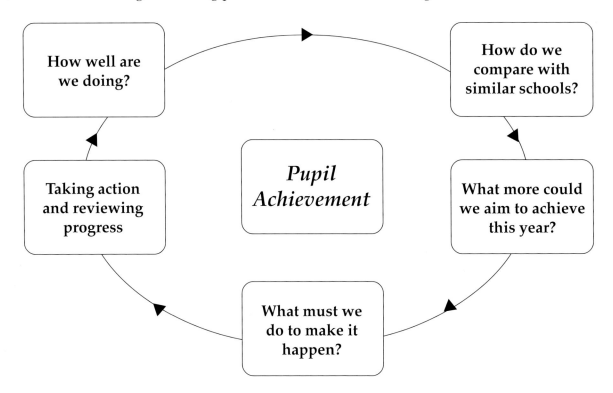

As teachers do not work alone, schools cannot hope to raise achievement without making sure that everyone who is involved in the process of target setting actually helps. This argument is continued in more detail in Chapter 6 but, by considering some of the stages of the cycle, suggestions for ways in which the roles of different colleagues can help to raise achievement by being involved in the culture and ethos of school improvement are provided here.

How well are we doing?	✔ Pupils have to be given the opportunity to discuss their work with their teachers.
	✔ Teachers must collect and analyse data about individual pupils' performance.
	✔ Subject co-ordinators should review standards across the school in their subject as part of their monitoring and evaluation role.
	✔ The headteacher should be in a position to look critically at current achievements and analyse trends.
	✔ There should be an obligation on both parents and teachers to discuss how each child is performing.
	✔ Governors should be able to ask challenging questions about the school's performance within a positive climate which encourages school evaluation and review.
How well should we be doing?	✔ Pupils should work within a supportive environment which encourages them to ask themselves questions about how well they should be doing.
	✔ Each teacher needs to be able to look at each of the children in his or her class and set specific targets related to their achievement. This is reviewed against previous targets and previous knowledge of their ability.
	✔ Subject co-ordinators must analyse the performance of similar cohorts and previous cohorts.
	✔ Senior managers should compare current and previous results against those from similar schools.
	✔ Parents need to be in a position to tell their child how well he or she is performing.
	✔ Governors need the information that will help them to understand how the school's performance compares with schools locally and nationally.
What should we aim to achieve this year?	✔ The ethos of the school must encourage children to have high expectations.
	✔ Teachers must have the time and the forum for playing a full part in target setting and forecasting pupils' future attainment.
	✔ Subject co-ordinators should help teachers to forecast pupils' future attainment.
	✔ The headteacher and senior managers must help to set realistic and challenging targets for improvement.
	✔ Parents have to understand what their child's targets are and be shown what kind of support is needed to secure his or her achievement.
	✔ The governors, after a full discussion, must agree the targets set by the school.

What must we do to make it happen?	✔ Children need to know what the targets are and how they are going to achieve them, the detail of which will depend on age. ✔ Each teacher should determine the range of actions within the classroom which need to be taken to improve individual pupil performance and the performance of the group and the cohort. ✔ If there are whole-school issues related to the action that needs to be taken, co-ordinators need to be in a position to take action. ✔ The headteacher must be seen to be taking determined action to improve achievements. ✔ Parents should work with their child to achieve the targets. ✔ The governors must have the kind of overview that makes sure that plans are in place to meet the targets focused on classroom practice.
Taking action and reviewing progress	✔ All pupils need to work in an environment that encourages them to maintain positive attitudes and work hard. ✔ All teachers must implement the agreed curriculum and all action plans that have been developed to meet targets and raise achievement. ✔ Co-ordinators need to work alongside teachers to confirm or revise individual pupils' end of key stage targets. ✔ The headteacher and his or her senior managers must continue to monitor and evaluate the actions that are being taken to improve pupil performance. ✔ The governing body should continue to check that targets are properly monitored and reviewed.

A co-ordinator working alongside a teacher to revise a pupil's targets.

In Appendix A, there are useful handouts which deal with some aspects of target setting and which could be used for staff development.

The whole-school approach

This chapter has emphasised the importance of target setting and, at the same time, made it clear that targets alone will not raise achievement. Each teacher in each school has to have action plans that will help individual children to reach their targets and the school to raise its own achievements. The rest of the book provides some techniques and suggests how they can be used. But, as was emphasised in Chapter 1, an individual teacher cannot work alone; there needs to be a whole-school approach involving decisions on:

✔ how the school is organised
✔ what effective teaching actually is
✔ how teams of teachers can help to raise achievement
✔ the important role of the headteacher in the whole process.

Chapter

3

The whole-school approach

It is easy to say and may sound far too simplistic, but we have to recognise that schools do make a difference. There are schools that are effective, where standards and levels of attainment are consistently good, and, unfortunately, there are schools where this is not happening and standards remain low. It is far beyond the scope of this book to identify and analyse why this should be so, but there are opportunities to recognise and suggest some of the reasons why some schools are more effective than others.

Effective schools make a difference

The background

Let's start in the late 70s and 80s. When members of the committee which later produced the Elton Report (1989) visited schools, they recognised the variations in 'feel' or atmosphere between different institutions and were convinced that 'some schools had a more positive atmosphere than others' (p.88).

Rutter et al. (1979) had also reached tentative conclusions about the influence of schools and the fact that some schools were actually better at raising achievement and were seen to be more effective than others. He suggested:

> 'It is not argued that schools are the most important influence on children's progress, and we agree ... that education cannot compensate for the inequities of society. Nevertheless, *we do suggest that schools constitute one major area of influence, and one which is susceptible to change'* (p.182) (my italics).

Rutter's arguments, which were probably some of the first words in the 'effective' schools movement, suggest that schools can, through their own good practice and effectiveness, raise the standards and levels of pupil achievement.

Mortimore et al. (1988) suggested a now fairly standard list of what needs to be in place in a school in order to create a positive atmosphere that will contribute to raising standards. Their influential book, *School Matters: The Junior Years*, describes how they carried out research in fifty schools and asked fairly simple questions about whether the school actually made a difference to pupil achievement and whether certain characteristics led to more effective schools.

Characteristics

They suggested that, in order to achieve effectiveness and improved pupil achievement, the following characteristics will help:

- ✔ There must be effective and powerful leadership.
- ✔ The deputy headteacher needs to be involved in all major decisions.
- ✔ All teachers need to feel that they are part of the decision making process.
- ✔ There needs to be consistency and continuity throughout the school in terms of discipline patterns, homework policies, resource management, timetable structures, standards of teaching and so on.
- ✔ Teaching sessions need to be structured, matched to children's needs, well paced and lively.
- ✔ The actual teaching should be intellectually challenging for all pupils.
- ✔ The environment of the school should be task and work oriented, that is every pupil should recognise that learning is the norm rather than the exception.
- ✔ There should be constant communication between teachers and pupils both inside and outside the classroom.
- ✔ Record keeping and assessment need to be sensible and thorough and communicated to parents when necessary in a way that they can understand.
- ✔ There should be a positive climate where emphasis is placed on praise rather than criticism.
- ✔ Control in classrooms must be firm but fair, with children being treated as individuals.
- ✔ Activities should be organised to take place outside the classroom and away from the school. This is a means of offering pupils wider experiences and a way of putting the academic content of the curriculum into a different context.

The message to schools is unequivocally clear: they have the power, through the efforts of the head, teachers and all those associated with the school, to raise standards of work and raise achievement. To do this, however, improvements may have to be made and changes may have to take place.

Making changes to improve the school

The list of the characteristics of effective schools is important. If certain of them are missing, it is more than likely that your school is less effective than it could be and that the children in it are achieving less than they are capable of doing.

It is interesting actually to break down the main ideas into more manageable issues. I would choose four headings: the headteacher, teachers, pupils and the school itself. It is in these four areas where change may have to take place.

The headteacher	An effective school which intends to improve pupil achievement needs a headteacher who:

✔ is open and approachable
✔ sets a good example
✔ has a good knowledge of the curriculum
✔ looks for ways to improve the school
✔ listens to parents
✔ is available in the school
✔ talks with pupils around the school
✔ is fast and effective at dealing with problems
✔ uses resources efficiently.

Teachers	An effective school which intends to improve pupil achievement has teachers who:

✔ participate in decision making
✔ make staff meetings useful
✔ organise their classrooms appropriately
✔ maintain discipline
✔ monitor pupils' progress and give regular feedback
✔ have high expectations of all pupils
✔ have classes that are well managed
✔ understand the needs of the pupils.

Pupils	An effective school which intends to raise pupil achievement has pupils who:

✔ are motivated
✔ are challenged by the curriculum
✔ have the necessary basic skills
✔ are encouraged to take responsibility and show initiative.

The improving school	If a school is being managed in order to improve pupil achievement, it will have identified the six following conditions that have to exist if staff are to achieve their goal of raising standards:

✔ Enquiry and reflection.
✔ Collaborative planning.
✔ Involvement of staff, pupils and governors.
✔ Staff development.
✔ Effective 'subject' co-ordination.
✔ Effective leadership.

Managing change

No schools are perfect and it is quite acceptable for the headteacher, teachers or senior managers to recognise that there are areas of the school that are less effective than others and, because of this, the quality of teaching and learning and the level of achievement are being impaired. If this is the case, then it is important to make changes. One of the major tests of the success of the school is the way in which it makes changes and manages the process. And, of course, if pupil achievement is limited, there has to be change.

Managing change is like solving a problem

One of the simplest ways of solving a problem is to:

✔ recognise what the problem actually is
✔ suggest why it exists
✔ state clearly what must happen if the problem is to be solved.

There are routines that may seem tedious, but, if they are followed, will make change easier to manage. They are really based on the simple idea that if schools want to improve, they have to recognise what needs changing and be prepared actually to do something about it.

Any change situation is a balance between two sets of forces. Some forces will be resistant to change and others will be positive driving forces which will help change to take place. It helps to think of a real example, such as 'there has been too little monitoring and evaluating of the Maths teaching and pupil achievement is suffering'.

Restraining forces that are resistant to change

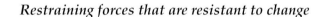
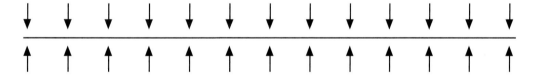

Driving forces that promote change

The first thing to do is to write down a description of all those people and circumstances that might either resist such a change or contribute to creating a situation that could make such a change difficult. These will be the restraining forces.

The next stage is to describe the people, reasons and circumstances under which the change could be promoted fairly easily. These will become the driving forces.

The process of managing change

If the restraining forces and driving forces have been identified in a thoughtful and structured way which involves everyone who has a vested interest in making the changes, it is less difficult to see the process through to a successful conclusion.

It is necessary, however, to continue the process in more detail. There are eight stages involved in planning the action that needs to be taken.

The stages of managing change

Stage 1
Recognise the problem, identify it and describe in writing the problem or the change that is needed. Don't just think about it.

Stage 2
Split the problem or change into:
    (a) the current situation, i.e. where we are now
    (b) the desired situation, i.e. where we should be.

Stage 3
List the driving and restraining forces. This will be easy because you will already have completed this part of the management of change.

Stage 4
Highlight those forces, both positive and negative, that are the most important.

Stage 5
Look at the restraining forces that have been highlighted; write them down and, alongside them, list all the actions that could reduce or eliminate them.

Stage 6
For all the driving forces that have been highlighted, list actions that would increase the force.

Stage 7
Work out from the responses to Stages 5 and 6 the most promising steps which could now be taken and identify the resources that are available.

Stage 8
Look closely at the most promising steps and place them in order of priority, using this as the final chance to omit any that will not work. It is important at this stage to set time limits for completing the change.

Characteristics of effective teachers

Change is ongoing and schools with an ethos which is aimed at raising standards and improving pupil achievement will manage the process well as a matter of course. Schools like this will have effective teachers who not only work well in the classroom but are a supportive part of the school's management. They will probably have the following characteristics:

✔ **Self awareness**
  They are aware of their own attitudes and values and how they affect other people.
✔ **Will to achieve**
  They constantly seek new challenges.
✔ **Optimism**
  They feel positive about the future and the part they intend playing in it.
✔ **Positive regard**
  They respond to others with warmth and respect.
✔ **Trust**
  They are prepared to trust their colleagues.
✔ **Empathy**
  They understand colleagues' points of view.
✔ **Courage**
  They are prepared to take risks to find more effective ways of working with colleagues.

Effective teaching

So far in this chapter, we have looked at the way in which schools can make a difference and some of the qualities that successful schools need. The role of the headteacher, co-ordinators, teachers and pupils has been examined briefly because it is important to have an adequate framework within which achievement can be raised. The main vehicle through which schools become or remain successful will be effective teaching. This is at the centre of all schools that are raising standards and improving pupil achievement. All teachers in a school, however, should be in agreement on the requirements for effective teaching. The following overview suggests the broad outlines.

Planning

There is a cliché which is worth remembering. It is: if you fail to plan then you plan to fail. It is essential to plan what you teach. In fact, within schools there should be a three-tier system of planning.

✔ The long-term planning sets out the curriculum map and identifies the key areas of the curriculum that are taught in specific year groups or key stages.
✔ The medium-term planning breaks this mass of material down into its National Curriculum components within a smaller block of time, such as six weeks or a term.
✔ The short-term planning reflects what is actually taught in the classroom.

There should be clear *objectives* set for each lesson and the main thrust of the lesson should be to make sure that all pupils know what the objectives are and how they will be taught and learned. To be able to plan objectives for a class and then to differentiate within the class for children of different abilities means that accurate *records* have to be kept of each pupil's progress. Planning the work for tomorrow means knowing where the pupil is today, and the only way of knowing that is by assessing pupils in as many ways as possible. It is also a good idea to plan *homework* that supports what is happening in the classroom, extends each pupil's knowledge and is differentiated in such a way that it is capable of being completed by all pupils.

Lesson organisation

Once the planning is complete and the objectives are clear, resources organised and homework set, it is absolutely vital that the way the lesson is taught is organised.

Each teacher has different personal quirks but there has to be a variety of *teaching styles* which includes whole-class teaching, group work and individual work. There need to be *high expectations* of pupils' capabilities and, of course, the means to challenge and motivate pupils always to do their best within an academic atmosphere. There also needs to be *pace and progression* within each lesson so that pupils always leave with new knowledge, understanding and/or skills.

Evaluation

In the planning section, it was suggested that records need to be kept so that you know what the next step is for each individual pupil. A simple way of helping you to assess progress and understanding is to make sure that you are a careful and consistent *marker* and that your marking makes it clear to the child your views on a piece of work, but that it also helps you to assess where the child is and where they need to go next.

Matching the tasks you set to the pupils' needs is also essential. There will be very little progression, and it is far less likely that you will raise pupil achievements, if the work they are given is too easy or too difficult.

Developing good teachers

During appraisal, and this may be easier to develop as appraisal becomes tighter and more geared to promotion and higher earnings, it is possible to discuss with teachers their strengths and weaknesses according to the broad outlines of effective teaching. Some teachers, for example, will be good planners, others may be experts at evaluation.

To counteract any possible weaknesses, it is important that the school has consistent policies and that each teacher is not only aware of the policies but is able and willing to follow them. A teacher's individual strengths need to be harnessed to develop similar strengths in all teachers. In order to raise standards, it is necessary to ensure that the standards of teaching are consistently high across all subjects. As well as the basic general outline of successful teaching, there are additional criteria for 'good' lessons that will raise standards. A 'good' lesson will enable a pupil to fulfil his or her potential and a 'poor' lesson is a lesson where pupils' potential remains unfulfilled.

Given below is a list which identifies various criteria for a successfully taught lesson.

An effective lesson

An effective lesson will include some or all of the following factors:

✔ Thorough planning with clearly identified objectives.

✔ A clear introduction which explains the objectives to all the children and a conclusion with the whole class to reconsider whether the objectives have been met.

✔ A well-organised classroom with clear behaviour expectations and consistently applied rules.

✔ A fast paced, enthusiastic and rigorous lesson.

✔ A variety of teaching methods including effective questioning.

✔ If it is appropriate, an emphasis on the importance of getting basic facts right, such as tables in Maths.

✔ Challenging work that motivates all pupils.

✔ Differentiation that matches the work to the ability of the pupils.

✔ Clear and defined opportunities for assessment of work with the aspects to be assessed stated clearly to all pupils.

✔ Opportunities to raise self-esteem and build confidence.

✔ Encouragement of pupils to think for themselves and ask questions.

✔ An understanding that no pupil is allowed to waste his or her time or that of the rest of the class.

✔ The provision of opportunities for children to take some responsibility for their own learning.

✔ Well-planned homework that is linked to the lesson content.

✔ Continuity between one lesson and the next.

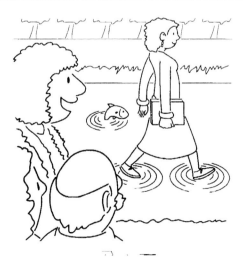

'She is so good, the children are unsure if this is Science or RE.'

There is a need for schools to formalise what they mean when they identify 'good' and 'bad' teaching. If there is a whole-school approach and whole-school staff development, it should be possible to create a cohesive set of criteria for identifying the kind of good practice that will improve attainment. This kind of approach will also reduce the negative influence of teachers who are not particularly good at what they do. It is important to recognise the characteristics of ineffective teaching. The following descriptions are provided in order that they can be avoided because they will act as barriers to change and will lower a school's chances to improve achievement.

A bad teacher

A bad teacher is one who:

✔ quite often frightens children and acts as a kind of adult bully

✔ creates tension based on the pressures of unrealistic goals and deadlines

✔ sees children and parents as threats and views parental help in a negative light

✔ emphasises punishment rather than praise, stress rather than calm, and hardly ever smiles or laughs

✔ has a style of control that builds up petty incidents out of proportion and has a similar level of punishment for all incidents, big and small

✔ often stifles enthusiasm and sees lively and curious children as a threat

✔ frowns on a wide curriculum and sees education in terms of a narrow range of basic skills

✔ sees outcomes as standard and stereotyped and develops a restrictive timetable that dominates every routine

✔ defines self-expression, the 'arts' and other forms of spontaneous creativity as not being 'work'

✔ has a suspicious attitude rather than an informed opinion towards change

✔ demands passive learning and has a single dominating teaching style that does not enable much effective differentiation

✔ often insults children and yet expects good manners and tolerance.

'And now a lesson on my role model: Vlad the Impaler.'

Chapter

4

Planning to raise achievement

In the previous chapter, planning was identified as one of the most important criteria for effective teaching, that is, the kind of teaching that is likely to raise standards and improve pupil performance. Whilst good planning cannot guarantee good teaching, it is rare to find good teaching which has not been well planned.

It is also unlikely that effective teaching and learning will be achieved unless all staff have a clear sense of direction and share a common planned curriculum that is appropriate to each year in the primary school.

The three strands

The three strands of planning: long, medium and short term, were introduced briefly in Chapter 3.

Long-term planning

This can also be called the school's curriculum map. It ensures that:

✔ all subjects of the National Curriculum, RE and other appropriate areas are properly covered
✔ there is progression in each subject at each key stage
✔ there is coherence within and between subjects, appropriate allocation of time, appropriate cross-subject links and continuity between key stages.

Schemes of work for each subject are the vital part of long-term planning.

Medium-term planning

Here, the long-term planning, the curriculum map and the scheme of work are broken down into smaller units. In many schools, these are half-term or whole-term blocks of time. It is difficult to specify how schools might develop their medium-term planning because mixed age classes, other kinds of vertical grouping, the use of specialist teachers and whether the primary curriculum is seen as subject based or better taught through cross-curricular themes determine how the specified blocks of time are used. But medium-term planning should certainly:

✔ set out specific learning objectives and the depth of treatment they are to receive
✔ identify the resources that are required
✔ link and reference the work to the National Curriculum and other units of work
✔ set out broad tasks and activities that children should be involved in
✔ suggest the kinds of differentiation that are expected
✔ indicate assessment opportunities.

Short-term planning

This is where teachers have to produce their own individual lesson plans which ensure effective day-to-day teaching and inform future planning. The balance between different types of activities and learning styles, day-to-day differentiation, appropriate pace, constructive feedback to children, assessment and monitoring and evaluation of progress is the responsibility of each class teacher.

In fact, 'good' short-term planning should enable each teacher to answer these questions:

✔ What are the purposes of my teaching?
✔ What activities will the children do to achieve these purposes?
✔ What resources do I need to allow these activities to happen?
✔ What finished work will emerge as a result of these activities?
✔ How can I assess the success of my teaching?
✔ Will my planned work fit into the time I have available?

Schemes of work

Why is a scheme of work necessary?

Putting it in its simplest terms, the scheme of work sets out what is to be taught. It tells teachers what they have to cover. The assumption is that, if the curriculum content of the scheme of work is taught well, it will, at its very least, maintain progress and, at its best, improve achievement.

These are the main functions of a scheme of work:

✔ To provide a measure of agreement, a framework within which to work.
✔ To help to promote continuity and progression.
✔ To create security and give confidence.
✔ To provide a model which can help to measure success or failure in terms of what is being taught, that is, the content of the curriculum.
✔ To confirm to staff the content of what they should be teaching.

What should a scheme of work contain?

Having a coherent policy for each subject is essential. Knowing the broad outlines of what is to be taught and how this will happen is vital if standards are to be raised and pupil achievement maintained and improved. The scheme of work is derived from the policy and gives detailed plans for teaching and learning that readily translate into classroom practice.

It is neither sensible nor justifiable for a scheme of work to be too prescriptive. Teachers need to have confidence in their own abilities to convert what they have to teach into their own creative classroom practice.

Despite this, in addition to some of the areas already suggested, such as continuity, coherence and progression, there are others that should be included in any scheme of work:

✔ Record keeping procedures.
✔ Assessment and evaluation procedures, including examples of children's work to indicate development and level of attainment.
✔ Links with other curriculum areas.
✔ Suggestions as to how commercial schemes fit into the school scheme of work.
✔ Resources to be used and their location including computer software.
✔ Lists of recommended books for teachers' personal reading.
✔ Lists of appropriate television broadcasts and video recordings.
✔ Suggestions for displays.
✔ Suggestions for marking pupils' work.
✔ Content guidelines, including an indication of the main knowledge, concepts, skills and attitudes to be addressed in each year.
✔ An approximate amount of time to be allocated each week.
✔ Suggestions for differentiated work for least able children.

Developing schemes of work

Individual schemes of work may be the responsibility of one person but they should involve teams of teachers and preferably, before they are finally accepted, the whole school. This is because poor schemes of work, or ones which are only fully understood by a single writer, will not sustain or improve your current test results.

Schemes of work also have a relatively short life cycle which has to involve the kind of monitoring and evaluation that recognises their built-in obsolescence and requires frequent changes and rewrites. It involves their being written, used for a period of time and then modified.

Criteria for successful lesson plans

Each teacher has to break down the schemes of work into teachable lessons which occupy a relatively fixed block of time. As well as recognising that individual lesson plans must be easily accessible so that they can be referred to quickly, they need to enable other teachers who might take the class to see what the children have done and what they should be doing next.

Lesson plans should ensure that there is a reduction in the degree of uncertainty to a reasonable level and an increase in the probability of children being provided with an appropriate level of high quality teaching.

Sometimes lesson plans are criticised for the length of time they take to create and this will continue to be a criticism as the curriculum becomes more complex and demanding. There is really no answer to this, except to say that it will remain a problem which can be best reduced by learning how to devote a minimum amount of time to maximum effect, so that full justice can be seen to be done to the educational needs of all the individuals in your classroom.

'That's Monday sorted!'

Levels of knowledge

Each school will have a slightly different method of writing lesson plans and it would be impossible to write a universal master plan here.

What is possible, however, is to suggest areas of knowledge that have to be covered and a checklist of criteria used in successful plans. First of all, each teacher needs to be aware, when writing a daily or weekly plan, that within these areas of knowledge, each level is progressively more difficult than the last one and, like climbing stairs, to get to the top – that is, reaching a high standard – each pupil has to tread on each step with all his or her intellectual weight.

Six levels of learning

Level 1: Knowledge

Each child recognises, learns and recalls information.

Level 2: Understanding knowledge

The pupil interprets, translates and summarises information.

Level 3: Applying knowledge

The child applies the knowledge and information gained in a situation different from the original learning context.

Level 4: Analysing knowledge

The pupil has the ability to separate blocks of information into parts and create new relationships.

Level 5: Synthesising knowledge and information

The pupil is able to form new relationships and combine knowledge and information from different areas to create new blocks of understanding.

Level 6: Evaluating knowledge

The child can take decisions and make judgements based on evaluating the knowledge and information that he or she has available.

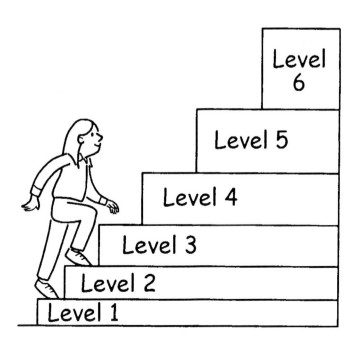

Differentiated lesson plans

If all children are to be given opportunities to learn by moving through the different levels of learning, then lesson plans have to reflect those opportunities. Some of the criteria that will help to achieve this include the following:

✔ Setting clear aims and objectives.
✔ Structuring the lesson in terms of blocks of time allowed for certain activities.
✔ Using appropriate teaching styles for different activities.
✔ Making it clear which resources will be needed, such as worksheet, TV and video.
✔ Organising the activities to include some for the whole class, some for groups and some for individuals.
✔ Setting out clear and achievable goals for the children.
✔ Writing brief notes on the kind of differentiation that will be used for both low achievers and the more able.
✔ Deciding what key questions will need to be asked and at what times in the lesson.
✔ Planning the homework that will be given to extend the work done in class.
✔ Indicating how today's lesson will link into other lessons.

Differentiation and match

A thorough and well-developed scheme of work together with the most successful lesson plan and the best teaching styles will not raise standards or improve attainment if there is little or no differentiation. It is difficult to ensure pace, rigour and challenge for able pupils while at the same time making sure that low achievers complete work with understanding and enjoyment. All primary teachers find matching the level of work to the abilities of their pupils difficult. This is understandable when they are teaching around thirty mixed-ability pupils.

The key to effective differentiation is to reject as unworkable any attempt to try to teach each pupil separately but, at the same time, to recognise that it is necessary to be aware of different ability groupings. When managing these groups within the classroom, it is also important that they are limited to three. Differentiated work can be provided for three groups without too many problems of classroom organisation and the needs of the most able at one end of the ability scale and the less able at the other should be able to be catered for.

To create differentiated groups, or any other method of differentiation, all teachers need to develop methods to find out where their pupils are now and to know what kinds of activities and approaches are likely to help pupils to take the next learning step and make appropriate progress.

Montgomery (1989) suggests that there are three ways of modifying teaching technique to achieve successful differentiation. They are:

✔ differentiation by giving more time
✔ differentiation by content level
✔ differentiation by personal contribution.

Differentiation by giving more time

If teaching is aimed towards the middle range of ability, the slower learners and lower attainers will experience difficulties and lose motivation. Most teachers will try to give these children more time. This is not particularly efficient, however, because the rest of the class will receive less time with the teacher and it is possible for the more able to complete tasks quickly, presenting further organisational challenges for the teacher.

Differentiation by content level

This is merely a form of streaming by ability within the same class. It is widely used because it limits the problems that pupils have with the material, as the material is geared to their abilities and needs and allows the teacher to spread attention fairly between all pupils.

However, the pupils will know who is being given lower level work and may regard this as lower status, so making this form of differentiation potentially divisive. Its success or failure in improving attainment will depend on the skills and attitudes of the teacher and, to some extent, the attitude of the school towards individual pupil needs and the sense of value placed in all pupils.

Differentiation by personal contribution

All pupils in the class are set the same task but the manner in which it is set and the strategies used for its completion, together with the acceptance of different outcomes, mean that individuals work at their own level. This approach relies on individual and group strategies and a co-operative atmosphere. It can avoid social divisions and overcome attention seeking and disruption, and all pupils should feel some kind of ownership of both the content of the curriculum and the processes they are going through. It is easier to follow in some subjects than in others.

Differentiation strategies

We will now look at some differentiation strategies in more detail and suggest some practical ways that they can be used in the classroom.

Some differentiation strategies

These are some strategies that could be used:

✔ Allowing for different levels of response.

✔ Altering the length of the task.

✔ Changing the vocabulary used.

✔ Asking different levels of questions to different pupils.

✔ Accepting different outcomes from a task that is common to all.

✔ Establishing different criteria by which success is measured.

✔ Varying the amount of knowledge, skills and understanding of the subject needed to enable a satisfactory response to be made.

✔ Varying the type of resource used.

✔ Varying the support given to individual pupils.

✔ Varying the time allowed for completion of the task.

Although there are many different teaching styles and techniques and many ways of organising a classroom to meet the demands of differentiation, two techniques seem to predominate and are given in *150 Ways to Improve National Curriculum Test Results* (p. 34):

✔ Differentiation by task where there are higher levels of more difficult work and lower levels of easier work.
✔ Differentiation by outcome where there is a whole-class task set for everyone, but different outcomes are expected.

Differentiation by outcome

Setting a task for the whole class and expecting different outcomes has many advantages for both teachers and pupils and few disadvantages.

Because the whole class can recognise that the same work is being set, they feel that they are being treated equally and that they can support each other in completing the same open-ended task. Each child is given an opportunity to show what he or she can do and the activity will offer opportunities for each child to show positive achievement. By its very nature, a whole-class activity of this kind will have to be open ended and some pupils find this kind of work more difficult than tasks that require more straightforward answers.

For teachers, however, setting the same task and expecting different outcomes makes it easier to differentiate between the various levels of attainment. It is also easier both to mark work that is set in this way and to organise resources. At the beginning of the lesson when the same task is introduced to the class, there are good opportunities for whole-class discussions, and well-structured questions that can be targeted at different levels for different pupils.

Differentiation by task

Setting work to match children's ability levels is more difficult to organise but is still an important technique to use. Stimulating tasks of different levels of difficulty and sophistication can be tailored to groups of children with different levels of ability. It can raise self-esteem because the tasks are achievable and this can stimulate children to achieve more as they are able to recognise their own successes.

But the tasks have to be precisely matched to the ability level of the group and it is important not to have too many different groups working on separate tasks within the classroom. Four groups is the maximum and three is more easily managed. Even with this number, there is the danger that some tasks will be too easy and this will not provide pupils with the opportunities to develop or demonstrate skills of which they are capable. There are also problems if the tasks set are too difficult. Self-esteem may be lowered, confidence may be undermined and the adults in the classroom may well find that they have to devote too much of their time to a specific group.

For the teacher, there is a lot of preparation if the tasks are to be set accurately for different ability levels. This will require a considerable amount of prior knowledge of pupils' abilities and the need to avoid expectations which are so rigid that they make it difficult for pupils to change between ability groupings.

Effective teachers see differentiation as an integral part of their work and the use of different strategies to enhance the learning of all their pupils is based on a deep understanding of the individual needs of the children in their class. The best and most successful differentiation is achieved by ensuring that progression is accomplished at an appropriate pace, and by encouraging group work using a variety of activities to enable all children to demonstrate their strengths.

Clearly, differentiation both by task and by outcome have their own strengths and weaknesses but a combination of the two styles is an excellent strategy for raising achievement and improving performance. Tasks which require a considerable amount of reading will almost certainly need differentiated resources even though the task is the same. Similarly, Maths tasks may deal with the same concept/process but different groups will handle different data. Open-ended writing tasks, such as one which requires children to write an account of an argument from two points of view, will be undifferentiated in the task but the teacher would expect very different outcomes from a typical primary class.

The use of homework

Using homework can raise standards. It needs to be of the right quantity and of an appropriate quality. It can be used to extend the school day and increase the amount of school work that is completed. It can also emphasise the link between home and school, providing that it is not simply used to continue and complete classwork or is a type of undifferentiated 'blanket' homework that does not support raising achievement.

Homework

Homework can only raise achievement if:

✔ there is a homework policy that everyone follows with specified amounts of homework in terms of time for each year group

✔ all homework matches the pupils' ability

✔ all homework is marked

✔ parents are made aware of the homework that is set through home–school links, such as homework diaries or home–school books

✔ the homework is useful and is an extension of the class work rather than simply a set of revision activities that the child can already do

✔ specific homeworks are set to develop skills in completing national tests

✔ it is set regularly so that both parents and children know when it will be sent home and when it needs to be returned

✔ care is taken that homework is not set which some children cannot complete at home because they have not got the appropriate resources, such as research from books that may not be available, the use of the Internet, the need for a computer version of Encarta or an expectation of a level of literacy support that some parents may not be able to offer.

Chapter 5

Using specific strategies

In earlier chapters, we have discussed target setting, effective teaching, whole schools working as teams, how planning can affect achievement, differentiation and the use of homework as strategies for raising standards.

We now need to make four assumptions:

✔ Firstly, that each subject area has clear policies, guidelines and schemes of work in place.
✔ Secondly, that teachers use these to plan their lessons.
✔ Thirdly, that their subject knowledge has been supported and developed through meetings and staff training and development.
✔ Fourthly, that there are sufficient resources as well as suitable teaching spaces both to maintain standards and improve achievement where it is appropriate.

Nevertheless, the question always remains: is it all going to work and can improvements be made? The answer to this is yes, providing there is no let up in the move to raise standards. A position will never be reached where teachers, senior managers and the headteacher and governors can say that they have achieved all that is possible. There are always new ways forward and better ways of teaching and managing the curriculum. Successful schools always have the broad target of raising achievement in mind as well as strategies that will help them actually to do it.

Possible strategies

One way of reducing the possibility of complacency and any tendency to stand still is to identify certain strategies and to use them as regularly and as consistently as necessary. Good schools are able to diagnose precisely what they need to change in order to deliver improvements and to use certain strategies unfailingly. These strategies can involve:

✔ constantly reinforcing core values
✔ looking at pupil progress
✔ questioning whether specific teaching methods are actually appropriate
✔ constantly raising questions about classroom discipline and relationships with pupils
✔ using teachers' individual skills effectively
✔ preparing for the tests that are a major way for parents to judge the school's achievements.

Core values

Core values are fundamental to all teachers of whatever age and whatever specialism. Every governor, every headteacher, senior manager and teacher should have as their most important target these core values. It has to be stressed that these values apply to all teachers, classroom assistants and lunch-time supervisors. They are shared values and the target to raise achievement will not be met unless everyone shares them and delivers the same messages to colleagues, children and parents.

Core values, by their very nature, are simple and relatively short. They are linked to raising achievement, to the need to improve teaching and learning and the need to meet targets related to these areas.

Core values for meeting targets and raising achievement

Teaching must always involve:

✔ well-paced lessons

✔ high expectations

✔ challenge, motivation and differentiation

✔ continuous assessment of individual children and the class against school targets and targets set for individuals.

Pupils must:

✔ be given opportunities to learn new skills and develop existing ones

✔ know each lesson's objectives

✔ have targets set that are achievable but not too easy

✔ make definite progress towards their targets over a set period of time.

Class and curriculum organisation will always include:

✔ well-planned lessons

✔ differentiated homework

✔ knowledge of ability levels of the less able and more able children in the class.

Measuring pupil progress

When targets have been set, policies and schemes of work are in place, lesson plans are clear with tight learning objectives and effective teaching has been a vital part of the staff development agenda, you need to examine the outcomes of all the work and effort that has been put in to raise standards.

When you do this, you are asking questions about what children really learn rather than what we think we teach. Gadsby and Harrison, in *The Primary Co-ordinator and OFSTED Re-inspection*, suggest that: 'A monitoring sweep of the actual work pupils produce in written and pictorial form can provide a very powerful tool of monitoring and evaluation. Written work produced by a sample of pupils from Reception to Year 6 in your school provides little hiding place in terms of standards and progression.' (p.129)

Monitoring the progress of children by using a sample of written work from across the age ranges will help you to make judgements about both their progress and their attainment.

Progress

In examining *progress*, these are some of the questions you might ask:

- ✔ Is there too much repetition or too little reinforcement of learning?
- ✔ Is there real, agreed evidence of improvement in quality, quantity and mastery of skills from one age range to the next?
- ✔ Does the learning that is taking place in specific age ranges represent an appropriate challenge to the children's range of needs and abilities?
- ✔ Are children gaining in knowledge, skills and understanding?
- ✔ Are they applying their learning in different situations?

Attainment

In examining *attainment*, these are some of the questions that need to be asked:

- ✔ Are the appropriate National Curriculum levels of attainment being reached at appropriate ages?
- ✔ What differences in attainment are there between boys and girls, children from different ethnic groups and so on, and if any are significant, what steps are being taken to make changes?
- ✔ Are those children who have been targeted to reach Level 2 at age seven with support and Level 4 at age eleven with support actually receiving that support?
- ✔ Is there obvious progression in attainment at appropriate levels?

There is a growing and probably continuing tendency for the inspection process to be increasingly driven by perceived outcomes. The work that children produce on a regular and daily basis is the most important and informative output and it will accurately reflect the quality of the school's policies, plans, teaching and targets.

Using effective teaching methods

In the OFSTED *Handbook for the Inspection of Schools: Amendments* (1994), it was noted that, in unsatisfactory lessons, no actual teaching was done by the teacher, who acted mainly as a supervisor of, or service to, individuals or groups; there was poor management and use of time in lessons, often with no deadlines being set and/or wastage at the beginning and end of lessons; and there was an overuse of undifferentiated worksheets. Inspectors also noticed that the tasks set were insufficiently challenging or dull, often as a result of poor management and control of pupils, that there was poor organisation and management of resources, and that the aims and objectives set for the lessons were unclear and often led to unsuitable tasks for the children.

Lesson observation   In setting targets to raise achievements, it has to be assumed that teaching is effective. Unsuccessful lessons must be minimised. One way to do this is for co-ordinators, senior managers and headteachers alongside supportive local authority advisers/inspectors to observe and monitor teaching directly.

Direct classroom observation should allow questions to be asked about:

✔ teaching methods
✔ classroom organisation
✔ control and discipline
✔ relationships within the class.

The National Curriculum, individual and whole-school targets, national testing and a purely judgemental inspection process have created a need for the close scrutiny of how teachers work in their classrooms. At the same time, tensions and dilemmas in teaching are proliferating and teachers are wrestling with a variety of these dilemmas within their classrooms.

Some of these include:

✔ when to teach individual children and when to teach the whole class
✔ when to direct all the learning that takes place, or when to allow children to take decisions about what they are doing
✔ when to use strict and rigid control and when to be more open and relaxed
✔ when to demand precisely delineated outcomes and when to accept open-ended results
✔ when to work with the whole class, with groups or with individuals.

Questions to raise

These are some of the questions that might be raised during lesson observation:

✔ Were the teaching methods appropriate for the age of the children?
✔ Was the subject matter appropriate?
✔ Were the resources that were used and that were available suitable?
✔ Was the teacher comfortable with the teaching methods and styles of teaching that he or she was using?
✔ Did the teaching method(s) take into account the varying levels of ability in the class?
✔ Was it possible to modify the approach, pace and level of the work?
✔ Were styles and methods changed when attention was lost by some of the children?
✔ Was appropriate questioning that was linked to ability levels used as part of the overall teaching method?
✔ Was it obvious that the teacher was comfortable when teaching the whole class, small groups and individuals?

Several of the questions relating to teaching methods ask about the appropriateness of certain actions for the age and ability of the children. This is because, despite setting general school targets and even individual attainment targets, it is still important to remember that the children in your class need to be able to relate to what is taught, to recognise its relevance to them, to have their imaginations stimulated and to feel motivated to learn.

Classroom organisation

Classroom organisation has always been important because it is the central means through which the educational aims and targets are translated into practice. This presents quite a technical problem for teachers because it involves the construction of a coherent classroom strategy by which space, children, time, resources, tasks and activities can be co-ordinated, and this, in itself, is a highly skilled activity. The following questions need to be asked:

✔ Is the layout of the room in terms of furniture, space, practical areas and book corners suitable for both the children and the teaching method being used?
✔ Is the grouping of children appropriate and likely to lead to progress?
✔ Are children given some responsibilities for the way they organise their work?
✔ Is there clear progression built into the lesson which provides opportunities for different outcomes?
✔ Are resources organised in such a way that they are accessible to children and do not always need the teacher to organise them?
✔ Do the classroom displays reflect work in progress and the range of achievements in the classroom?
✔ Has each child got a personal space for his or her belongings?

No one single method of classroom organisation will always lead to maintaining and improving standards. Having said this, however, well-organised classes enable rather than hinder effective learning. Classroom organisation must respond to the needs of the teacher and the class, to the work they have to do and to the space and resources that are available.

The decisions that are made about classroom organisation will have a major effect on the running of the class and on the quality of teaching and learning that takes place. In many ways, the manner in which classrooms are organised is a significant indicator of the degree to which the school's attainment targets will be met.

Classroom discipline

An initial skill for teachers is to create the most productive learning environment possible for the majority of co-operative children. Unfortunately, the word 'co-operative' does not apply to all pupils and teachers also need to develop the ability to respond to the time-consuming number of incidents of disruptive behaviour that may take place in many classrooms.

The central challenge for teachers is to devise strategies that will pre-empt such behaviour, or increase the ability to respond to it in a way that is not damagingly stressful to the teacher and harmful to the learning of other pupils in the class. These are some of the questions, suggested by Gadsby and Harrison (p. 139), that can be asked about discipline and relationships with pupils:

- ✔ Is there a calm, relaxed atmosphere in which learning can flourish?
- ✔ Are pupils expected to co-operate with each other?
- ✔ Can the teacher manage and control pupils in a variety of situations?
- ✔ Are there obvious strategies for coping with conflict and for solving individual problems?
- ✔ Is the pace appropriate and the differentiation such that there is little conflict and frustration caused by failure and lack of self-esteem?
- ✔ Does the teacher show an awareness of the differences between groups and individuals?
- ✔ Are there clear and precise instructions?
- ✔ Is there mutual respect between teachers and pupils and between pupil and pupil?
- ✔ Is there a framework of clear and sensible rules?
- ✔ Do pupils demonstrate an understanding of classroom rules?
- ✔ How does the teacher react to children who break the rules?
- ✔ Is the teacher aware of what is happening in the classroom?
- ✔ Are their rewards as well as sanctions?

Is there a calm, relaxed atmosphere?

Obviously, classroom discipline and control are important. Without them, classrooms will not function, children will not learn and attainment targets will not be met.

But control and discipline need not be seen as purely negative although, at the time, severe incidents of disruption may well make the teacher see the world in a less than positive light. The exercise of control and discipline should be a habit and not a sudden happening. Constant monitoring and vigilance using a consistent tone of voice, words and body language will engender mutual respect. Without such respect, a disciplined class becomes much more difficult to achieve.

Looking at the way in which teachers and children relate in a classroom is a very useful method of gathering evidence about the possible achievements of that class. Such observations may reveal both a child's ability and his or her attitude to learning. It may tell us that some children are not being given the conditions under which they can develop, grow and reach their potential. To achieve school targets, as has been pointed out already, individual children have to reach their own targets. A child's performance provides both the raw data of his or her ability as seen in test scores and teacher assessments, and information on how that ability is harnessed, sustained and reflected in the reality of day-to-day classroom and school life.

Individual pupils

Level of attainment

Teachers need to know as much about individual pupils as possible so that they can teach them at a level that is appropriate to their learning needs and make sure that they progress through the curriculum. At the end of their infant and primary education, in Year 2 and Year 6, each individual pupil's level of attainment will be part of the school's overall target. It is vitally important, therefore, that each child's level on his or her national test score can be predicted accurately from as early an age as possible.

Knowing that a child is going to get Level 4 at eleven and Level 5 with some extra support makes it important to be able to put in that extra support in terms of better and more differentiated homework or more small group work based on ability levels. But, if the percentage of children reaching Level 4 at eleven is going to rise, it is important to know which children will not get Level 4 unless there is some dedicated intervention. This intervention cannot just take place from September in Year 6 but has to have been in place since, at the latest, Year 3. Each teacher needs a profile of each pupil so that the teaching and the school's resources can be related directly to an individual's needs.

A pupil's profile

A profile of each child should include most, if not all, of the following:

✔ All the child's previous test results including:
  – base line assessment
  – Key Stage 1 national test results
  – school practice tests available for Years 3–5
  – any internal tests such as for Reading

✔ Teacher assessments

✔ Predicted levels from past teachers

✔ Predicted present level

✔ Report comments that will or will not support the present level

In discussing a cohort of children with colleagues in order to set targets, it is also important to be able to recognise the strengths required to succeed. It is of little value to state that certain pupils might achieve Level 4 with support if it is known that their attitude to school and their general level of behaviour will not help them to make such improvements. These kinds of barriers to raising achievement will be discussed in Chapter 6, but here are some of the strengths required of pupils who are likely to progress and whose achievement is likely to be raised.

Required strengths

Pupil strengths needed to improve achievement will include:

✔ a keenness to ask questions as well as answer them
✔ the ability to gain information from texts and to understand what is being read
✔ good time management and the ability to use time well and complete work on time to the required standard
✔ a good vocabulary and a range of views on different subjects as well as a wide general knowledge
✔ good social skills and the ability to make and sustain friendships
✔ an ability to memorise facts as well as solve problems
✔ an ability to persevere in the face of adversity.

Test results

Obviously, setting targets to raise achievement is not just about improving test results but equally obviously, the higher the national test scores are, the better. Poor scores which should be better will result in parental dissatisfaction and lack of support which may result in children leaving and an inevitable cycle of poor, if not poorer, scores. Low test scores will help no-one and will certainly not support those higher values of setting both wider academic and social targets to raise the overall standards of all children in all curriculum areas. Poor test results and lack of confidence will not help to raise achievement in Art, PE or RE. A good football team and strong athletics skills usually come from a school that has deeper strengths and a sound academic core.

So it is very important to know what the tests are like and to make some preparations in order that children succeed in them. This is especially true when you consider that certain factors will have an impact on test results. These include:

✔ knowing what an actual test paper looks like
✔ knowing what different kinds of questions mean
✔ knowing how to link what the children know and what they have been taught to different kinds of questions
✔ being able to work to a time limit and at the same time produce good results
✔ being accurate and not making avoidable errors.

Preparing for tests

It seems rather obvious that the more preparation there is, the easier it is to be successful. There is also a cliché that practice makes perfect. Accepting the need to practise is fine but every school and every teacher must not lose sight of the fact that they have to make sure that they also deliver a broad and balanced curriculum.

There is also a law of diminishing returns on preparation and practice for national tests. Too much can make the children tense and even stale. They need to peak at the right time, not three months earlier.

Test analysis

First of all, tests and the test results can be analysed from previous years, preferably *the* previous year by asking questions such as the following:

✔ Were there identifiable easy and difficult questions?
✔ Which did teachers feel were the best questions that suited their children?
✔ What modifications might be needed to the schemes of work because of the types of questions?
✔ Were all the expected topics on the test paper?
✔ What topics were there that have to be covered lower down the school and repeated in later years?
✔ Did the test raise any implications for staff development in terms of whole-school curriculum issues?

Past papers

Once this analysis has been completed, it has to be put to some use. In other words, the past papers can be used as practice tests to help this year's children to achieve better levels of attainment. This is useful because the pupils are put under the pressure of a 'real' test situation, they are able to see and use a real test format, they can experience test conditions and they become aware of the absolute time constraints of a test. At the same time, teachers can identify pupils' strengths and weaknesses when dealing with a 'real' test situation, identify priorities for revision, and predict individual results more accurately, in order to find out which children will reach higher levels with some additional input of some kind.

What it will also suggest is whether using the optional tests in Years 3–5 was helpful, whether base line and Year 2 national test results have any bearing on Year 6 scores and whether the results obtained from the optional tests help to predict the likely scores at eleven. They might also suggest that, for some children, the barriers against success are so severe that the school's targets are made lower because such children are not expected either to help the general process of raising standards or to raise the levels of attainment in the national test scores. These issues of non-attainment and barriers to success will be part of the next chapter.

Chapter 6

Removing barriers

Apart from the short section on discipline and relationships in the classroom, there has been little mention of the negative factors in schools which can prevent standards being raised. The fact that certain factors exist which make raising achievement difficult does not mean that we should assume that schools facing such difficulties should give in. We should always remember that effective schools with effective teachers do make a difference.

What makes a difference?

School Matters: The Junior Years by Mortimore et al. has already been used to provide evidence of the characteristics that actually make a difference. These include:

✔ strong leadership
✔ effective teaching
✔ good resources
✔ a positive school environment

and when they are present, they can enable a school to produce results and improve achievement that overcome most of the disadvantages and barriers it faces.

It is, of course, much harder work and there must always be the feeling that any targets set are always on the edge of being met or not met, because there are fewer guarantees of success in schools which have formidable barriers to raising standards.

School atmosphere

The Elton Report (1989) uses the phrase 'school atmosphere' (p.89) and emphasises that there were 'differences in a school's feel or atmosphere' (p.88) and that 'perhaps the most important characteristics of schools with a positive atmosphere is that pupils, teachers and other staff feel that they are known and valued members of the school community' (p.90). They go on to suggest, fairly predictably, that schools can have a positive or a negative atmosphere and equally that schools with a negative atmosphere will suffer more from those barriers to learning such as bad behaviour, poor attitudes, inability to concentrate and low parental support than those with a positive atmosphere. Symptoms which suggest a negative atmosphere, and which themselves will lead to low expectations and poor standards include:

✔ widespread litter
✔ long-standing graffiti
✔ teachers starting lessons late and finishing early
✔ teachers ignoring bad behaviour in the playground
✔ the use of inappropriate punishments and rewards.

Throughout the book, the emphasis has been on how the school and the teaching can affect standards and how poor leadership, attitudes to change, lack of subject co-ordination and bad teaching can create barriers to development. There has been very little discussion on the barriers to achievement associated with the pupils.

Unexpected factors

Pupils fail in some areas of the curriculum, or do not perform as well as they should, for a variety of reasons. If we assume that sensible targets have been set and that the teaching is effective there are, unfortunately, pupils who will not meet their targets, or have had to be set lower individual targets than are appropriate.

Possible reasons

Here are some of the reasons for this to happen:

✔ Special needs from Stage 2 upwards.
✔ Poor attendance, including unauthorised absences and a high incidence of lateness.
✔ Poor behaviour and an inability or refusal to accept school rules.
✔ Low self-esteem and a permanent sense of failure.
✔ Poor socialisation skills so that there is often conflict at home, with the teachers and with peers.
✔ Lack of parental support or even the rejection by parents of what the school and education have to offer.
✔ Family changes, such as divorce, separation or death in the family.
✔ Lack of participation in anything the school offers, including after-school clubs, sports and so on.

Some of these barriers may prove to be intractable but others can be influenced by the positive action of the school and of other agencies which can co-operate to assist families and individuals to succeed.

There are excellent local schemes for improving attendance and punctuality. Good School Support Teams and Educational Psychologists can work closely with staff to improve behaviour.

Self-esteem is critical and there is much published in the field. A number of relevant recommended publications are listed at the end of the chapter.

It is obvious that academic targets for raising achievement need support from other targets, such as improving attendance, reducing the number of late arrivals and incidences of unauthorised absence, and raising the numbers of children who participate in extra-curricular activities.

To some extent, the barriers in the list can be seen as out of the school's and the teachers' hands. For example, a difficult separation which affects learning and attitudes can occur suddenly and be hard to manage. A death in the family can be totally unexpected but have a devastating effect on a child's learning. This means that such incidents cannot be planned for except in as much as teachers need to be able to deal with these situations by having a wide range of skills available to them.

Known factors

There are other more predictable barriers which are known about individual children from an early age but which, nevertheless, can affect how individual targets are set and can lower the school's achievements. But, because they are easily recognised, strategies can be developed to overcome them.

Possible barriers   These are some of the 'known' barriers to a child's learning and achievement:

- ✔ Being slow to settle down in class.
- ✔ Being easily distracted and constantly distracting other children.
- ✔ Copying other children's work.
- ✔ Often failing to complete homework.
- ✔ Preferring to gossip rather than listen.
- ✔ Not responding particularly well to praise.
- ✔ Completing work quickly and at a superficial level.

Both the barriers that are largely unexpected and those that are known represent attitudes to learning that are either already present or begin to develop because of some incident that has occurred at home and in the family.

The attitude of children to learning can be more powerful than any innate ability and measurable intelligence and can determine, to a great degree, their behaviour in the classroom and how much they will benefit from the teaching that takes place.

Pupil attitudes

Obviously, children with a positive attitude to learning will exhibit good behaviour, get on with their peers and relate well to their teacher. They will be interested in the work that they are asked to do, be able to sustain concentration and will always be involved in tasks set by the teacher and tasks that they set themselves. They are model pupils and can and should be used as examples to children with less well-developed, positive attitudes.

Negative attitudes are difficult to overcome. Setting high achievement targets for children with negative attitudes will not usually help the school to improve its attainments. This is because, unless the negative attitudes are changed to positive ones, it is unlikely that such a child will benefit from any extra support that either teachers or classroom assistants can offer.

Negative attitudes

Here are some of the negative attitudes in pupils that have to be overcome in order to raise achievement:

✔ An unwillingness to apply themselves to tasks.
✔ A refusal to join in discussions.
✔ An unwillingness to persevere to complete tasks or to solve difficult problems.
✔ A lack of enthusiasm.
✔ A lack of pride in any of their work.
✔ A difficulty in participating in group work, especially co-operative group work.
✔ An inability to share resources including their own and those belonging to the class.
✔ An inability to learn from mistakes.
✔ A hatred of making mistakes of their own but quick to laugh at the mistakes of others.
✔ An inability to work without the direct supervision of a teacher.

The roles of those who can break down barriers

Poor attitudes to learning present teachers with considerable barriers when they set out, as they do each day, to improve the quality of their teaching and the learning of their pupils. Many people have roles to play in breaking down the barriers that have been described. Teachers are at the centre of this process. I have tried to describe earlier some of the effective practices that make up 'good' teaching and that, by implication, will raise standards.

Teachers are extremely skilled but are not always their own best publicists when it comes to stating their roles in raising achievement. Schon (1983) raises an interesting point by describing the skilled actions of teachers as 'knowledge in action'. What he means is that teachers can often demonstrate in action what they are doing but find it difficult to verbalise or describe it. In other words, 'good' teachers can teach well, that is they can demonstrate their teaching and classroom management skills and all the other wider roles, but have difficulty in actually stating what it is that makes them effective practitioners who overcome learning barriers on a daily basis.

'I know what I am doing but I find it hard to put it into words.'

In examining the roles of most of those who are involved in breaking down and removing the barriers to learning so that targets can be set and improved achievement can take place, I will use the same subheadings that I used earlier. These relate directly back to Chapters 1 and 2 where target setting and benchmarking were discussed and include the following sequence of ideas:

✔ How well are we doing?
✔ How well should we be doing?
✔ What should we be doing to achieve more?
✔ Taking action and reviewing progress.

The role of the teacher

Effective teaching has a major role to play in breaking down barriers to improving achievement and it is important for teachers to look closely not only at their class as a whole but also at individual children. By doing this, each teacher will be able to add his or her knowledge of a particular group of children to the school's target setting process, to the whole-school plan to raise achievement and to the planning discussions for any future major curriculum changes.

How well are we doing?	✔ Collect and analyse data about the individual performance of all pupils, paying particular attention to underperforming and high achieving pupils.
	✔ Use previous data that has been collected, including discussions with previous teachers to identify strengths and weaknesses.
	✔ Report the information to subject co-ordinators, senior managers and the headteacher.
	✔ Share any relevant information on targets and progress with pupils, where appropriate, and parents.

How well should we be doing?

✔ Review and analyse the pupils' present attainment against their previous achievements.

✔ Compare their performance against any available national data.

✔ Discuss and analyse the data on specific subjects with subject co-ordinators and other colleagues.

✔ Explain to parents the purposes of target setting and the terms 'attainment' and 'progress'.

What should we be doing to achieve more?

✔ Forecast pupils' future attainment based on knowledge of the pupils and on evidence of past achievements.

✔ Have high expectations of the children in the class.

✔ Ask individual pupils questions, such as 'How could you do better?', 'How can I help you?'

✔ Help pupils, bearing in mind their age and maturity, to understand target setting.

✔ Give pupils the chance to talk about their own targets and be involved in setting them.

✔ Take a full part in using the knowledge of your class to decide cohort and school targets.

✔ Involve parents and help them to understand their child's own targets.

✔ Contribute work from your children to the portfolio of moderated work.

✔ Make sure that the knowledge of the children's past attainments and future targets informs teaching and learning.

Taking action and reviewing progress

✔ Implement action plans to meet agreed targets.

✔ Monitor individual progress and achievement.

✔ Review and revise individual targets as a result of monitoring individual progress and achievement.

✔ Evaluate the effectiveness of teaching strategies.

✔ Keep appropriate records of achievement and progress.

The role of the subject co-ordinator

The role of the subject co-ordinators in primary schools is extremely important. Not only do they carry out a delegated responsibility on behalf of the headteacher but they are class teachers, leaders and administrators. Their role is central to the development and management of the curriculum and how it is taught.

They are expected to be fully aware of the current position of their subject in relation to the overall curriculum management of the school, as well as knowing past achievements and setting targets for future and better achievements. Each co-ordinator, and this is especially true for those who have responsibility for the core subjects of Maths, English and Science, must be closely involved with class teachers and their individual and class targets as well as able to advise senior managers and the headteacher on cohort and school targets in their specific subject.

How well are we doing?

- ✔ Review standards across the school.
- ✔ Discuss the findings with colleagues and with senior managers and the headteacher.
- ✔ Record the findings as evidence for the specific year and specific classes and year groups.

How well should we be doing?

- ✔ Discuss and analyse subject performance of present classes and cohorts against previous performance and previous cohorts.
- ✔ Analyse school performance in subjects in relation to national and local data including benchmarks.
- ✔ Present the analysis to colleagues, senior managers and governors.

What should we be doing to achieve more?

- ✔ Hold meetings to help teachers to forecast pupils' future attainment.
- ✔ Lead staff development on specific subjects.
- ✔ Raise expectations where necessary.
- ✔ Co-ordinate the provision of portfolios of moderated work.

Taking action and reviewing progress

- ✔ Identify whole-school issues which act as barriers to subject development.
- ✔ Suggest or develop school policy on what needs to be done to improve pupil attainment.
- ✔ Support staff in raising achievement in specific subjects.
- ✔ Confirm or revise individual pupils' targets including those for the end of Key Stages 1 and 2.
- ✔ Review schemes of work and make changes.
- ✔ Monitor whole-school performance and report to the headteacher, colleagues and governors.

A list of publications which provide helpful suggestions for achieving some of these tasks is given at the end of the chapter.

The role of the headteacher

Good schools have effective leadership and a positive climate. The headteacher is central to creating the kind of positive ethos that will break down barriers to learning. To do this, he or she will have to be skilful at managing resources and communicating ideas to everyone associated with the school. An awareness of the need for continuous improvement will, through his or her skills of administration, target setting and effective teaching and learning, go hand in hand with vision, foresight, faith and imagination.

Purposeful leadership, while maintaining the professional involvement of teachers, is a careful balancing act and becomes even more of a complex tightrope when parents and governors are involved. Headteachers have to be aware of the role teachers play in school improvement and have to be able to articulate this role, its effectiveness and the kinds of targets that can be expected to a wide-ranging audience which starts in the school with colleagues, governors and parents but which also extends outwards to LEA inspectors and officers and OFSTED inspectors.

How well are we doing?

- ✔ Identify and analyse trends in attainment and targets.
- ✔ Help teachers and co-ordinators to analyse their data and set targets.
- ✔ Ask whole-school questions, such as 'Are some groups doing better than others and if so why?'
- ✔ Meet with teachers, co-ordinators and governors to discuss data and share targets.
- ✔ Report to governors, LEA and OFSTED the school's targets together with the evidence on which the targets are based and the performance of the cohorts, past and present, that go together to create the whole-school targets.

How well should we be doing?	✔ Consult with subject co-ordinators and teachers. ✔ Review current performance against local and national information. ✔ Compare the school with the performance in similar schools. ✔ Present data to governors in a meaningful way that helps them to understand the school's position.
What should we be doing to achieve more?	✔ Establish a system for collecting teacher forecasts for their pupils' performance. ✔ Establish a system for collecting subject data from subject co-ordinators. ✔ Check that this data is realistic and achievable and challenge teacher forecasts where and when necessary. ✔ Agree targets with teachers and subject co-ordinators. ✔ Create a broad range of other non-academic targets. ✔ Take account of the broad range of abilities of pupils when agreeing and setting whole-school targets. ✔ Set targets which are SMART: Specific, Measurable, Appropriate and Agreed, Realistic and Recorded, and Time related.

Taking action and reviewing progress	✔ Ensure that Action Plans are drawn up which specify:
	  – what will be done
	  – who will be responsible for doing it
	  – what resources and support will be needed including staff development
	  – what the timescale will be
	  – who will monitor progress
	  – what evidence there will be to evaluate success.
	✔ Inform governors of progress to meet targets at appropriate intervals.
	✔ Ensure that progress towards targets is discussed with all senior managers.

The role of the governors

Governors have considerable power and, if they exercise this power, they will be able to exert a significant influence over how successful the school is. They have a statutory duty to be involved in the preparation of any curriculum statements, schemes of work, policies and the achievement targets the school sets itself.

For governors to play a full part in developing these targets, they must be involved in discussions on how they have been reached. This must happen openly without the staff keeping back unpalatable information, such as the number of low achievers in a particular class, and the governors should, on their part, work towards establishing positive and open relationships. This kind of relationship does not, however, mean that governors must simply accept what the staff is prepared to share with them. They must know how the school works, who the teachers are, what the catchment area is like, what the past levels of achievement are and they must be prepared to ask challenging and searching questions about how achievement can be raised, what needs to happen and what barriers there are to making it happen.

How well are we doing?	✔ Create a positive climate in which challenging questions can be asked.
	✔ Consider, with the headteacher, how the school's performance compares with its previous performance and whether some parts of the school are more effective than others.
	✔ Receive information early enough about how the school is performing so that decision making can be influenced.
	✔ Look at a range of indicators of pupil performance, such as pupils' attitudes.

How well should we be doing?	✔ Ensure that staff have the data to know how well they should be doing.
	✔ Look at the local and national performance of pupils and have an understanding of the school's performance against this data.
	✔ Look at wider benchmarking information, for example comparing pupils' attitudes to school with attitudes of pupils in similar schools.
	✔ Put the school in context, but keep the expectations high.
	✔ Compare attainment in different subjects.
	✔ Ask critical questions, such as 'Are we amongst the best schools of our type?'

What should we be doing to achieve more?	✔ Work with the headteacher and teachers to agree targets and publish them in the Governors' Annual Report to Parents.
	✔ Agree the allocation or reallocation of resources for the delivery of the targets.
	✔ Agree additional school or LEA targets.
	✔ Raise expectations.
	✔ Ensure that the targets are realistic and manageable.

Taking action and reviewing progress	✔ Make sure that plans are in place to meet the targets and that the plans are focused on classroom practice.
	✔ Check that targets are properly resourced.
	✔ Agree how progress can be monitored.
	✔ Ensure that progress towards targets is discussed at governing body meetings as a regular item on the agenda.
	✔ Ask challenging questions, for example:
	– Are we achieving the identified targets?
	– Are we in line with our estimated timescales?
	– If the targets were not met, how could we do better next year?
	– Were the appropriate resources identified and delivered?
	– If we are doing better than expected, should the targets be raised?

Some final thoughts

Target setting is an essential tool in improving achievement. Pupil performance targets add clarity and focus to any attempt to raise standards. Targets alone, however, will not do this. There needs to be a climate of positive thinking about school improvement and a commitment from teachers continually to improve their skills at raising the achievements of individual children and at setting targets that are acceptable to teachers, parents and governors.

— Features of acceptable targets —

✔ They are unambiguous and everyone understands them.

✔ They are valid and are likely to have a beneficial effect on the move to raise standards.

✔ They are achievable and everyone agrees that they can be achieved.

✔ They are manageable within any current restraints within the school and there are not too many targets which require too much time.

✔ They are measurable and it is possible to tell whether progress has been made.

✔ They are someone's responsibility and are linked to a delegated person.

✔ They are time limited and there is an obvious end point for each individual target.

'OK, are the targets quite clear?'

Recommended reading

From the Folens Primary Professional Development series:

✔ *Able and Gifted Children* by Chris Webster
✔ *Circles of Friends* by Colin Newton and Derek Wilson
✔ *Curriculum Leadership in the Primary School* by Steve Harrison and Ken Theaker
✔ *Family Literacy and Learning* by Mike Walton

From the Daniels Folens series:

✔ *Raising Self-Esteem* by Murray White

APPENDIX A: USEFUL HANDOUTS

———— Principles of target setting ————

TARGETS SHOULD:

✔ be challenging and raise standards for all

✔ be SMART:
- – Specific
- – Measurable
- – Appropriate and Agreed
- – Realistic and Recorded
- – Time related

✔ take into account the content within which the school and the children are working

✔ be based on sound evidence, supported by useful national and LEA benchmarking information

✔ reflect and reinforce priorities in the School Development Plan

✔ inform the LEA Educational Development Plan and contribute towards DfEE requirements

✔ meet the statutory requirements but also extend into recognition of achievement in other areas

✔ be set far enough in advance to be meaningful

✔ be monitored regularly

✔ fit into a cycle of school improvement which involves the following five stages:
- – Analysing current performance
- – Comparing results with similar schools
- – Setting the actual targets
- – Planning the action
- – Taking action and reviewing progress

✔ require a balance of pressure and support for success

✔ be set so as not to disadvantage any individual pupil or group of pupils in order that a school may meet its overall targets

✔ be set in a positive climate created by the headteacher and governing body which overcomes caution and leads to the adoption of challenging yet realistic targets within the school.

The five-stage cycle of school improvement and the roles of the key players

Target setting should put the performance of pupils, both their academic performance and other performance, at the centre of the school's work. The model which can underpin target setting is the 'Five-stage cycle for school self-improvement' which builds on the process already used by many schools for school development planning.

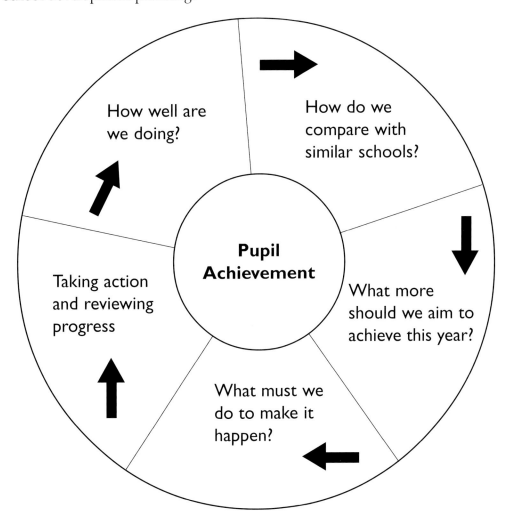

Setting targets involves governors, the headteacher, staff and the LEA working together, embedding the targets in the school's approach to planning and taking determined action to ensure success. It also involves pupils in taking responsibility for their own learning, with, wherever possible, parental support.

Class teachers in primary schools have an additional role to play in gaining an overview of each pupil's achievement in all areas of school life. They will be able to look for patterns of achievement, underachievement and overload. In addition, they are the people most likely to gather information and set targets in areas such as attendance, behaviour, involvement in clubs and other extra-curricular activities.

Examples of whole-school targets other than academic attainment

Schools will undoubtedly want to set targets for aspects of school life other than academic attainment. In some cases, schools will not have evidence of current achievement in a particular area and will have to carry out an activity to establish the base line against which they can set a target for improvement. Some examples of whole-school targets are given below:

Attendance

For example: 92% attendance

Behaviour

For example: Less than x detentions in the school year
Less than y exclusions in the school year
Reduction by 20% of parental complaints about behaviour
Reduction by 50% of incidents reported by lunch-time supervisors

Effort

For example: 80% of pupils receiving at least one commendation for effort in the school year

Attitudes

For example: 70% of pupils feeling that all their teachers enjoy teaching
Reduction by 20% of reported cases of racial harassment

Pupil satisfaction

For example: 90% of pupils feeling happy at school
80% of pupils being satisfied with the education that they are receiving

Pupil–teacher relationships

For example: 85% of pupils feeling that their teacher listens to them
All pupils relating well to at least one teacher

Participation in extra-curricular activities

For example: All pupils, during their time at the school, taking part in a residential activity
50% of pupils taking part in out-of-school clubs and activities
All pupils participating in an art, drama, music or sporting activity

Parental participation in open days/parent–teacher conferences

For example: Increase of 20% in the number attending

Target setting – Year .....

Class:	KS1 TA							KS2 forecast		
Name	**En**		**Ma**	**Sc**	**En**		**Ma**	**Sc**	**En**		**Ma**	**Sc**
	Re.	Wr.			Re.	Wr.			Re.	Wr.		
								Total at L4+				
								% at L4+				
								Total at L5				
								% at L5				

Targets for end of Key Stage 1

Class or group name: _____

Pupil details				Base line		TARGETS FOR ATTAINMENT AT THE END OF KEY STAGE 1								
						Reading			Writing			Mathematics		
Surname	Forename	Date of Birth	Sex	Summary Score	Perf. Group	as set in reception	as reviewed at Year 1	as reviewed at Year 2	as set in reception	as reviewed at Year 1	as reviewed at Year 2	as set in reception	as reviewed at Year 1	as reviewed at Year 2

Targets for end of Key Stage 2

Class or group name: _____

TARGETS FOR ATTAINMENT AT THE END OF KEY STAGE 2

| Pupil details | | | | KS1 levels | | | Y4 test | | English | | | | | Mathematics | | | | | Science | | | | |
Surname	Forename	Date of Birth	Sex	En	Ma	Sc	En	Ma	as set in Year 2	review in Year 3	review in Year 4	review in Year 5	review in Year 6	as set in Year 2	review in Year 3	review in Year 4	review in Year 5	review in Year 6	as set in Year 2	review in Year 3	review in Year 4	review in Year 5	review in Year 6

Number of pupils @ Level 4+ _____
% of pupils @ Level 4+ _____

Number of pupils @ Level 5+ _____
% of pupils @ Level 5+ _____

APPENDIX B: REFERENCES

Bearne, E. (ed.), *Differentiation and Diversity in the Primary School* (Routledge, 1996)

Bell, L. and Rhodes, C., *The Skills of Primary School Management* (Routledge, 1996)

DfEE, *Excellence in Schools* (DfEE, 1997)

DfEE, *From Targets to Action* (DfEE, 1997)

DfEE, *Setting Targets to Raise Standards: A Survey of Good Practice* (DfEE/OFSTED, 1996)

Elton Report, *Discipline in Schools: Report of the Committee of Enquiry Chaired by Lord Elton* (HMSO, 1989)

Gadsby, P. and Harrison, M., *The Primary Co-ordinator and OFSTED Re-inspection* (Falmer, 1999)

Kent Consultants, *150 Ways to Improve National Curriculum Test Results* (Kent Consultants, 1998)

McGuiness, J., *Teachers, Pupils and Behaviour: A Managerial Approach* (Cassell, 1993)

Montgomery, D., *Managing Behaviour Problems* (Hodder and Stoughton, 1989)

Mortimore, P., Sammons, P., Stoll, L., Lewis, D. and Ecob, R., *School Matters: The Junior Years* (Open Books, 1988)

North Tyneside Council, *A Team Approach to School Improvement* (North Tyneside Council, 1997)

Playfoot, D., Skelton, M. and Southworth, G., *The Primary School Management Book* (MGP, 1989)

Pollard, A. (ed.), *Children and their Primary Schools* (Falmer, 1987)

Rutter, M., Maughan, B., Mortimore, P., Ouston, J. and Smith, A., *Fifteen Thousand Hours* (Open Books, 1979)

Saunders, M., *Class Control and Behaviour Problems* (McGraw Hill, 1979)

SCAA, *Target Setting and Benchmarking* (SCAA, 1997)

Schon, D., *The Reflective Practitioner* (Basic Books, 1983)

Smith, R., *Successful School Management* (Cassell, 1995)

Smith, R., 'What makes a good teacher?', *Child Education* (November, 1998)

Southworth, G. (ed.), *Readings in Primary School Development* (Falmer, 1994)

Warwickshire County Council, *Target Setting in Schools* (Warwickshire Education Department, 1998)